I0154305

State of New York Legislature

Proceedings of the Senate and Assembly of the State of New York

Held in Relation to the Death of Reuben E. Fenton

.

State of New York Legislature

Proceedings of the Senate and Assembly of the State of New York
Held in Relation to the Death of Reuben E. Fenton

ISBN/EAN: 9783337159061

Printed in Europe, USA, Canada, Australia, Japan

Cover: Foto ©Suzi / pixelio.de

More available books at **www.hansebooks.com**

In Memoriam.

Reuben E. Fenton.

PROCEEDINGS

OF THE

SENATE AND ASSEMBLY

OF THE

State of New York,

IN RELATION TO THE DEATH OF

REUBEN E. FENTON,

HELD AT THE

CAPITOL, APRIL 27, 1887.

ALBANY:

WEED, PARSONS AND COMPANY

1887.

In Memoriam.

PROCEEDINGS

Legislature of the State of New York

ON THE DEATH OF

Ex-Governor Reuben E. Fenton.

IN ASSEMBLY :

MARCH 18, 1886.

Mr. BATCHELLER offered, for the consideration of the House, resolutions in the words following :

WHEREAS, REUBEN E. FENTON, who died at his home in Jamestown, Chautauqua county, on the twenty-fifth day of August last, was, for many years, a Representative in Congress, and for two successive terms Governor of this State, and afterward a Senator of the United States, and had occupied other important posts of trust in his own country, and as a representative of the National Government upon a special mission in Europe ; and

WHEREAS, During his extended and honorable public career, he achieved great distinction for himself and rendered enduring service to the State and to the Nation, especially by his loyal and unremitting devotion to the volunteer soldiers of the Republic during the eventful and trying period of the Rebellion; and,

WHEREAS, It is becoming that the State should place upon its public records its appreciation of such distinguished sons, and express a fitting tribute to their memory; therefore, be it

Resolved (If the Senate concur), That in the death of ex-Governor REUBEN E. FENTON, the State has lost an exalted patriot and a distinguished citizen.

Resolved, That the name of REUBEN E. FENTON shall be inscribed upon the archives of the State as one of the honored statesmen of the Republic.

Resolved, That these proceedings be entered upon the Journals of the Senate and Assembly, and that a copy thereof, duly engrossed, be presented to the respected widow of the deceased.

Resolved, That this House do now adjourn.

Mr. SPEAKER put the question whether the House would agree to said resolutions, and they were unanimously adopted by a rising vote.

IN SENATE:

MARCH 25, 1886.

The Assembly sent for concurrence the following resolution:

WHEREAS, REUBEN E. FENTON, who died at his home in Jamestown, Chautauqua county, on the twenty-fifth day of August last, was, for many years, a Representative in Congress, and for two successive terms Governor of this State, and afterward a Senator of the United States, and had occupied other important posts of trust in his own country, and as a representative of the National Government upon a special mission in Europe; and

WHEREAS, During his extended and honorable public career, he achieved great distinction for himself and rendered enduring service to the State and to the Nation, especially by his loyal and unremitting devotion to the volunteer soldiers of the Republic during the eventful and trying period of the Rebellion ; and

WHEREAS, It is becoming that the State should place upon its public records its appreciation of such distinguished sons, and express a fitting tribute to their memory ; therefore, be it

Resolved (If the Senate concur), That in the death of ex-Governor REUBEN E. FENTON, the State has lost an exalted patriot and a distinguished citizen.

Resolved, That the name of REUBEN E. FENTON shall be inscribed upon the archives of the State as one of the honored statesmen of the Republic.

Resolved, That these proceedings be entered upon the Journals of the Senate and Assembly, and that a copy thereof, duly engrossed, be presented to the respected widow of the deceased.

On motion of Mr. VEDDER, and by unanimous consent, the resolutions were made a special order for Monday evening, April 5, 1886.

APRIL 5, 1886.

The PRESIDENT announced the special order of the day, being the Assembly resolutions relative to the death of REUBEN E. FENTON.

Mr. VEDDER offered, in connection therewith, the following resolution:

Resolved (If the Assembly concur), That a committee of three be appointed on the part of the Senate, and a like committee on the part of the Assembly, to select an orator and to name a day for the delivery of an oration on the life and character of the late Hon. REUBEN E. FENTON, and to make all needful preparations therefor.

The PRESIDENT put the question whether the Senate would agree to said resolutions, and they were unanimously adopted by a rising vote.

The PRESIDENT appointed as such committee on the part of the Senate, Messrs. VEDDER, FASSETT and PARKER.

IN ASSEMBLY:

APRIL 6, 1886.

The Senate returned the concurrent resolution relative to the death of REUBEN E. FENTON, with a message that they have concurred in the passage of the same.

8

The Senate sent for concurrence a resolution in the words following:

Resolved (if the Assembly concur), That a committee of three be appointed on the part of the Senate, and a like committee on the part of the Assembly, to select an orator and to name a day for the delivery of an oration on the life and character of the late Hon. REUBEN E. FENTON, and to make all needful preparations therefor.

The PRESIDENT appointed as such committee on the part of the Senate, Messrs. VEDDER, FASSETT and PARKER.

Mr. SPEAKER put the question whether the House would agree to said resolution, and it was unanimously adopted.

Mr. SPEAKER appointed as such committee on the part of the Assembly, Messrs. BATCHELLER, CHENEY and J. HAGGERTY.

Ordered, That the Clerk return said resolution to the Senate, with a message that the Assembly have concurred in the passage of the same.

IN SENATE:

APRIL 6, 1886.

The Assembly returned the Senate resolution that a committee of three be appointed on the part of the Senate and a like committee on the part of the Assembly, to select an orator, and to name a day for the delivery of an oration on the life and character of the late Hon. REUBEN E. FENTON, and to make all needful preparation therefor, with a message that they have concurred in the passage of the same, and have appointed as such committee on the part of the Assembly, Messrs. BATCHELLER, CHENEY and JAMES HAGGERTY.

IN SENATE:

APRIL 14, 1887.

Mr. VEDDER offered the following:

WHEREAS, A joint committee on the part of the Senate and Assembly was appointed during the session of 1886, to select an orator to deliver an oration on the life and character of the late REUBEN E. FENTON; and

WHEREAS, The Honorable CHAUNCEY M. DEPEW was chosen such orator; therefore,

Resolved (if the Assembly concur), that Wednesday, April 28, 1887, at eight o'clock in the evening, be the time, and the Assembly Chamber the place for the said obsequies.

Resolved, That the Assembly be requested to appoint a committee to confer with the Senate committee to perfect further arrangements for the above-named ceremonies.

The PRESIDENT put the question whether the

Senate would agree to said resolution, and it was decided in the affirmative.

IN ASSEMBLY:

APRIL 14, 1887.

The Senate sent for concurrence a resolution in the words following:

WHEREAS, A joint committee on the part of the Senate and Assembly was appointed during the session of 1886 to select an orator to deliver an oration on the life and character of the late REUBEN E. FENTON; and

WHEREAS, The Hon. CHAUNCEY M. DEPEW was chosen such orator; therefore

Resolved (if the Assembly concur), That Wednesday, April 27, 1887, at eight o'clock in the evening, be the time, and the Assembly Chamber the place for the said obsequies.

Resolved, That the Assembly be requested to appoint a committee to confer with the Senate committee to perfect further arrangements for the above-named ceremonies.

Mr. SPEAKER put the question whether the House would agree to said resolution, and it was determined in the affirmative.

Mr. SPEAKER appointed as such committee on the part of the Assembly, Messrs. ERWIN, PLATT, FROST, SHEEHAN and DICKEY.

Ordered, That the Clerk return said resolution to the Senate, with a message that the Assembly have concurred in the passage of the same, and have appointed a like committee on the part of the House.

IN ASSEMBLY:

APRIL 27, 1887.

The Assembly Chamber held another distinguished audience this evening, when the legislative exercises in memory of the late ex Governor REUBEN E. FENTON were held. Many members of the Senate and Assembly, and State officers, with their wives, were present. The space back of the Speaker's desk was draped with the American colors, in the center of the festoon being a portrait of Governor FENTON. Senator COMMODORE P. VEDDER called the assemblage to order, and Speaker HUSTED was chosen to preside. Prayer was offered by the Rev. WALTON W. BATTERSHALL, D. D., of Albany, after which the orator of the evening, Hon. CHAUNCEY M. DEPEW, delivered a characteristically eloquent address on the life, character and services of Governor FENTON. Among those present from Jamestown, N. Y., the home of the late Governor, were Mayor O. F. Price, R. E. Fenton, Jr., the only son of the deceased, F. E. Gifford and Albert Gilbert, Jr., sons-in-law of Governor FENTON.

Remarks of Senator VEDDER:

Citizens and Members of the Legislature:

You know the purpose for which we have met. A great man, in the fullness of honor, has fallen in the midst of his people. To his virtues, manliness and genius we bear witness in this formal manner, and to his memory we pay the respect of a public funeral. A noble friendship, victorious over death, will attest, and eloquent lips will tell to-night the inspiring story of his eventful life. In this behalf, I am instructed by the joint committee of the two Houses to name a gentleman to preside who is himself a distinguished statesman, and who was the friend of him whose life and services we are met to commemorate, and, in obedience to such instruction, I have the honor to introduce the Honorable JAMES W. HUSTED, of Peekskill, N. Y.

Speaker HUSTED, upon taking the chair, was received with hearty applause. He spoke as follows:

Gentlemen of the Legislature:

We are met to do honor to the memory of one of the Great War Governors of New York, and to pay the fitting meed of Praise to the distinguished dead. As representative, executive and senator, he reflected upon the State the greatness and nobility of his genius and his patriotism. You have chosen, as his orator, the one of all others, who, by reason of his personal gifts not only, but as well from his intimate acquaintance with the subject of his eulogy, is eminently qualified to recount in glowing words his deeds and fame. I take great pleasure in presenting to you the Honorable CHAUNCEY M. DEPEW.

MEMORIAL ADDRESS

BY

Hon. CHAUNCEY M. DEPEW.

The Address.

Gentlemen of the Senate and Assembly of the State of New York:

New York has as a rule been remarkably fortunate in her Governors. Many of them have been statesmen of national and commanding influence. Two of them have served as Presidents and two as Vice-Presidents of the United States, and two others were the choice of their party for the Chief Magistracy of the Republic. Their influence upon the policy and course of government has been potential. It is proper in this place to speak only of those who have joined the majority beyond the grave. There is no more heroic figure in revolutionary annals than our first Governor, George Clinton. Within an hour after his inauguration he was marching to the post of duty and danger in front of the enemy. His obstinate courage, wise generalship and great popularity, did much to keep New York, full as the colony was of royalists, loyal to liberty and the Continental Congress. John Jay did

17

more than any one save Alexander Hamilton
to bind the discordant colonies into a harmonious confederacy. DeWitt Clinton by his
foresight and energy made New York the Em-
pire State, and her chief city the commercial
metropolis of the continent.

Martin Van Buren for nearly a quarter of
a century was the actual ruler of the Republic, through his control and management of
the dominant party, and he gave political
form and substance to the anti-slavery senti-
ment. William L. Marcy, United States Senator and twice a Cabinet Minister, has left
an indelible impress upon the history of his
time. Silas Wright ranks among our ideal
statesmen. He possessed the loftiest character
and most signal ability. His ambitions were
always subordinated to the public welfare.
He could calmly lay aside the certainty of
the Presidency when his duty, as he understood it, called him to serve in more hazard-
ous but minor fields, and he was in every
sense a modern Cincinnatus. The name of
William H. Seward will be among the few
of his generation which will survive in coming
ages. He was the political philosopher of
his period who alone of his contemporaries
grasped the full meaning and inevitable re-

sult of the vast moral questions which agitated the country. His matchless genius for affairs and unruffled judgment in the midst of trial and danger kept that peace with the world without, which alone enabled nationality to win its victory within. His speeches and state papers will be the exhaustless treasury from which the statesmen of the future will draw their best lessons and inspiration. Within our immediate memory the tablets upon our gubernatorial mausoleum recall the public services of John A. King, John A. Dix, Edwin D. Morgan, Horatio Seymour, Reuben E. Fenton and Samuel J. Tilden. No other State has been governed by an equal number of men of national influence and fame. It is, therefore, eminently proper and wise that the Legislature should commemorate and, by imposing ceremonial, perpetuate the history and characters of its departed Chief Magistrates.

EARLY TRIALS AND SUCCESSES.

The one in whose honor we are here assembled worthily ranks with the best of his predecessors in office. Repeated and long-continued promotions to places of trust by popular suffrage are cumulative evidence of merit and distinction. The opportunity to rise from hum-

ble station to lofty positions is the common
heritage of all, but they only successfully climb
the slippery and perilous ascent, gathering fresh
strength at each station for bolder efforts, who
are easily the leaders of their fellows. The
early settlers of Western New York were a
hardy and enterprising race, and their children
roughing it in log cabins, forest clearings and
frontier experiences, were by heredity and edu-
cation State builders. They created farms out
of the wilderness, formed communities and or-
ganized government. It is easier for a man
of ability to get on in a new country and
with fresh surroundings, than in the neighbor-
hood where he was born. Where everyone
has known him from childhood he often, is
handicapped by the unforgotten frivolities of
youth, and reaches middle life before he has
outgrown the feeling that he is still a boy,
while as a new settler he starts at once at
the level of his ascertained capabilities. It is
the peculiar distinction of Mr. Fenton that he
overcame these prejudices before he was of
age; that he became the choice of his fellow-
citizens for positions of trust as soon as he
obtained his majority, and passing his life at
his birthplace, he earned, at a period when
most young men are unknown, the confidence

of the people among whom he had grown up,
and carried it with him to his grave. He
saw Western New York expand from the forest into one of the most beautiful, highly
cultivated and richest sections of the State,
teeming with an intelligent and prosperous
population, which had founded cities, formed
villages, erected schools, endowed colleges and
planted by every stream flourishing manufac-
tories, and he remained throughout all this
growth, and until his death, the foremost and
most distinguished citizen. He was seven times
Supervisor of his town, and three times Chairman of the County Board, for five terms a
member of Congress, twice Governor of this
great State, United States Senator, and the
choice of New York for Vice-President in the
convention which first nominated General Grant.

This proud career was not helped by acci-
dent, or luck, or wealth, or family, or powerful friends. He was in its best sense both
the architect and builder of his own fortunes.
When a lad of seventeen his father failed in
business, and the boy dropped his studies and
professional aspirations to support the family
and retrieve its credit. Self-reliant but pru-
dent, courageous but cautious, his audacity
subject to reason, he quickly measured his

powers and then boldly struck out for himself.
He traversed the virgin forests, selecting with
unerring judgment the most productive tracts,
and for years following, his life was spent in
logging camps and piloting his rafts down the
Allegheny and Ohio rivers. The adventures,
exposure and perils of the work gave him an
iron constitution and knowledge of men, and
developed his rare capacity for business. An
omniverous and intelligent reader, he became,
by the light of blazing fires in the forest and
pine knots in the cabin on the rafts, well
educated and widely informed. At thirty-one
he had paid his father's debts and secured a
comfortable competence for himself. Then
came the inevitable internal struggle with himself of the man who has early in life achieved
an independence. He feels his strength, the
ardor and fire of vigorous manhood enlarge
his vision, and he sees no limits to his ambitions. The divergent roads to untold wealth
on the one side, or honors and fame on the
other, are before him, and to lead the crowd,
his best energies will be required for which-
ever path he selects. Mr. FENTON determined
to devote his future to the public service and
henceforward his life became identified with
the history of his times.

A LEADER OF THE NEW PARTY.

He had always been a Democrat, but the great question which was to destroy the Whig and divide the Democratic party, met him at the outset of his congressional career. Stephen A. Douglas had introduced into the bill organizing the territories of Kansas and Nebraska, a section repealing that portion of the Missouri Compromise of 1820, which forever prohibited slavery in the new territories lying north of latitude thirty-six degrees and thirty minutes. In a moment the whole country was aflame. The slumbering conscience of the Nation awoke with an energy which rocked pulpits, and revolutionized colleges. The oration, the tract and the madly exciting novel were potent forces in the storm. The young congressman must choose and at once between his convictions and the caucus. He did not hesitate. He was never afraid of his beliefs, and faith and courage with him always stood together. His maiden speech was for the inviolable preservation of the boundaries so solemnly set by a former generation to the encroachments of slavery. It was the first speech made from either side in the House of Representatives against the pending crime. It

was made by a member of the Party then dominant in the government, and its clear notes of
independence and defiance rallied about him a
determined band of young democratic representatives. From that day he was one of the
leaders in the formation and afterwards in the
conduct of the Republican party. When Mr.
Seward announced the death of the Whig and
christened the young party — Republican, and
when at its first State Convention there frater-
nized under that name, old Whigs and Demo-
crats, Barnburners of '48, Free-Soilers and
Liberty Party men of the days of Martyrdom,
REUBEN E. FENTON was unanimously elected as
their presiding officer.

It is difficult now to realize the duties and
responsibilities of a member of Congress during
the civil war. He was investigating estimates
and making appropriations of such appalling
magnitude, that he had no precedents to guide
him and no standards for comparison. Amidst
the tension and strain of great battles, of vic-
tories and defeats, of the result oft times in
doubt and the Capitol itself frequently in peril,
he was uprooting by legislation, wrongs and
abuses which had been embedded in the con-
stitutions, the laws, the decisions of the Courts,
as well as the approving judgment of the peo-

24

ple since the formation of the government, and preparing for the reconstruction of a new upon the ruins of the old Republic. Fundamental principles of human rights were pressing for immediate and final settlement, while the carnage, slaughter and suffering without and the financial and administrative perils within the Capitol were unparalleled in the experience of nations. But widely known and with a sympathetic heart he was counselor, friend and brother, for the mother searching for her dead, for wives looking for loved ones left wounded upon the field, for parents seeking furloughs for their boys in the hospital, that they might carry them home and tenderly nurse them back to life and health, and by the soldier's bedside he gave relief, encouragement and strength, or received the dying message and the last embrace to be tenderly borne to mourning and broken households in the peaceful valleys of the distant North. There were many men in Congress of commanding eloquence and great power in debate, who received general attention and applause, but Mr. Fenton did not excel in either of these more attractive fields. He was a man of affairs, one of those clearheaded, constructive and able business managers, whose persistent industry, comprehensive

grasp of details and power to marshal them
for practical results, made him invaluable in
committee where legislation is perfected and
all-important measures are prepared. The people rarely know the debt they owe to the
careful, plodding, alert members, who ceaselessly working in the committee rooms, with
no reporters to herald their achievements and
no place in the "Congressional Record" for
their work, detect frauds and strangle jobs,
mould crudities into laws and develop the
hidden meaning and deep-laid schemes of skill-
ful and deceptive amendments, ascertain the
needs of government and devise the statutes
for meeting them. They are the reliance of
the cabinet minister and the safety of parlia-
mentary government. There are always three
classes of Congressmen: the leaders who or-
ganize the forces of the administration or
opposition, and by speeches profound or mag-
netic give opinions to their party and educate
the country to its views; the able and con-
scientious committeeman and watchful member,
and the drones whose public usefulness is lost
between yawns and naps. Mr. FENTON was
an ideal representative of the second type,
with some of the qualities of the first. He
mastered his subject so thoroughly and under-

stood so well the causes and effect of pending issues, that his calm and lucid statements made him, upon the floor, a strong ally and a dangerous enemy. His speeches upon pensions, internal improvements, the regulation of emigration, the payment of bounties, the repeal of the Fugitive Slave Law, and the financial measures for carrying on the war, and funding the national debt, attest the extent of his acquirements and the wisdom of his views.

But his distinction during this period was, that he came to be preeminently recognized as the "Soldiers' Friend."

The bill to facilitate the granting of furloughs and discharges to disabled soldiers; the bill to facilitate the payment of bounties and arrears of pay due wounded and deceased soldiers, and bills granting pensions and those making the applications for them easy and inexpensive, were among the results of his patriotic and thoughtful interest. He kept lonely vigils by the hospital cots at night, and by day was ceaselessly and tirelessly tramping from the War and Navy Departments to the Executive Mansion.

The New York Soldiers' Aid Society, in recognition of his eminent fitness and meri-

torious services, elected him its president, and
the beneficent work of that society is recorded
in grateful hearts and registered by happy fire-
sides all over our State. When as governor
he welcomed home the returning regiments of
the disbanded army, the formal words of his
official proclamation spoke the sentiments which
had guided his actions. "Soldiers," said he,
"your State thanks you and gives you pledge
of her lasting gratitude. You have elevated
her dignity, brightened her renown and enriched her history. The people will regard
with jealous pride your welfare and honor,
not forgetting the widow, the fatherless and
those who were dependent upon the fallen
hero."

GOVERNOR OF NEW YORK.

The Presidential canvass of 1864 was one
of the most interesting in our history. The
radical element in the Republican party had
nominated a ticket after denouncing President
Lincoln because he was too slow and conserv-
ative. Governor Horatio Seymour, while voic-
ing the thought of the Democratic National
Convention, in one of the most able and
masterly of speeches, as its chairman, had declared that Mr. Lincoln's administration had

been a series of costly and bloody mistakes,
and under his guidance the war had been, and
would continue to be, a failure. To carry
New York, Mr. Seymour accepted a renomi-
nation for Governor, and entered upon the
canvass with his accustomed vigor and eloquence. Whether we differ from or sustain
his political opinions, we must all admit that
Horatio Seymour was one of the most bril-
liant and attractive of our New York statesmen. The purity of his life, his unblemished
character, his commanding presence, and his
magnetism upon the platform, made him the
idol of his party and the most dangerous of
opponents. It was vital to Mr. Lincoln and
his administration, and to Mr. Seward, the
chief of his cabinet, that New York should
sustain them and repel these charges. To meet
this emergency, and conduct this campaign,
Reuben E. Fenton was nominated by the Republican Convention for Governor. The wisdom of the choice was speedily apparent. Mr.
Fenton's unequalled abilities as an organizer
were felt in every school district in the Commonwealth, and when the returns showed the
State carried for Lincoln, and Fenton leading
by some thousands the Presidential vote, the
new Governor became a figure of national

importance. Within four days after his inauguration he raised the last quota of troops
called for from New York, with this stirring
appeal: "Having resolutely determined to go
thus far in the struggle, we shall not falter
nor hesitate when the rebellion reels under
our heavy blows, when victory, upon all the
methods of human calculation, is so near. Be-
lieving ourselves to be inspired by the same
lofty sentiments of patriotism which animated
our Fathers in founding our free institutions,
let us continue to imitate their bright example
of courage, endurance and faithfulness to prin-
ciple in maintaining them. Let us be faithful
and persevere. Let there be a rally of the
people in every city, village and town."

A few months afterwards the happy lot and
unique distinction came to him, following the
surrender at Appomattox, of being among the
immortals who will always live as the War
Governors of our civil strife; who in Thanks-
giving Proclamations, returned to Almighty
God the devout acknowledgments of a grateful people for the end of war and bloodshed,
and the victory of Unity and Nationality. That
he carried the State for his party at each
recurring annual election during his two terms
as Governor proves the popularity of his ad-

ministration and his skill as an organizer. By
temperament and training he was admirably
fitted for executive position. No one ever
understood better the peculiarities and surroundings of men. He was apparently the
most amiable and conciliatory of public officers, but never yielded an essential point.
He possessed in an eminent degree the rare
faculty of satisfying applicants and petitioners
without gratifying them. The immense State
and local indebtedness following the war, the
wild speculations incident to an unstable currency, and the perilous condition of public
and private credit he thoroughly understood,
and with great sagacity and judgment devoted
his powers to removing the dangers and preparing for the storm. He gave the State
what it most needed after the drain and de-
moralization of the civil war, a wise business
government. So profoundly impressed was the
convention which met at Syracuse in 1868,
to send delegates to the National Convention
at Chicago, with the strength of his administration that it unanimously and enthusiastically
instructed the delegates to present his name
for Vice-President, and for five ballots in that
memorable contest he was second on the
poll.

SENATOR OF THE UNITED STATES.

Senator Morgan realized, when it was too late to either gracefully retire or to avert defeat, that the power which Thurlow Weed had held for thirty years, and upon which he relied, had passed away and the Governor had become the master of the party forces in the State. Governor FENTON became easily the choice of the Legislature as Mr. Morgan's successor, and entered the Senate at a period when measures were pending which he thoroughly understood, and in their solution could render most valuable and enduring service. The bent of his mind was towards financial and business subjects, and the debt, taxation, the currency, banking and revenue were the pressing problems of the hour. No measures since the adoption of the Constitution have had such permanent and beneficial influence upon the growth and prosperity of the country as the acts relating to finance from 1869 to 1875. The national credit was impaired, the interest upon the debt was exorbitant and threatened the gravest complications, and *fiat* money induced the wildest speculation followed by its natural sequence, general bankruptcy and business suspension.

With rare courage and wisdom Congress declared that all the obligations of the Government should be paid in gold. Instantly the shattered credit of the Republic was restored and its securities advanced in all the markets of the world. Taking advantage of this good name and reputation, bills were passed funding the debt at a rate of interest so much reduced that a burden of over fifty millions of dollars a year was lifted from the taxpayers. Commerce, manufactures and all industries soon responded to this great relief, and the stability and healthy expansion of the vast business of the country were assured. But steady and reputable occupations, and the inauguration and completion of the enterprises which were in the years to come to develop in such a rapid and limitless way our exhaustless resources, were impossible with a fluctuating and uncertain currency. The full fruition of this grandest scheme of finance of modern times came with the resumption of specie payments. That the losses and destruction of the civil war have been regained, repaired and forgotten; that the Republic is many fold richer in every element of wealth, prosperity and promises for the future, are due to the wise foresight which prepared and perfected this harmonious and interdependent system. While Senator FENTON did his full share and occupied an honorable place in this grand and states-manlike work, he originated and promoted with all his ability, thoroughness and persist-ence the abolition of the moiety methods of collecting the revenue. The evils had long been apparent, but no one had the boldness to attack them. They originated when the young Republic was too poor to pay adequate salaries, and continued until the enormous receipts at the customs gave to the revenue officers a for-tune each year and retired them with large wealth. They were intrenched in the cupidity of incumbents and the hopeful dreams of aspi-rants. Those in possession and those who expected to be in the ever-varying tides of political fortunes were alike hostile to a change. The system was fecund in spies, informers and perjurers, and merchants were at the mercy of legalized blackmail. The final triumph of this beneficent reform will be remembered to his lasting honor.

FENTON AND GREELEY.

No record of Governor FENTON's life would be complete which failed to give the facts of his separating from his party for one campaign.

and no memorial honest which ignored its discussion. He supported the Republican candidates with all his might from the formation of the party till his death, with the single exception of his vote for Mr. Greeley; before this event bringing into the canvass all the forces of the organization then under his control, and after it, returning again within the regular lines, and giving his whole time and influence for the success in each succeeding canvass of Hayes, of Garfield and of Blaine. No organization was either large enough or elastic enough to hold in harmonious relations and views two such opposite, original and positive men as General Grant and Horace Greeley. All conditions in the beginning conspired to urge Greeley to independent action, as in the latter part of his canvass they united for his defeat. The rise of his tidal wave, until a vast majority of the voters were apparently drawn into the current, and then its sudden collapse, followed immediately by his sleepless watching for weeks by the bedside of his dying wife, brain fever, delirium and death, form one of the most dramatic episodes and romantic tragedies in American politics. Mr. Greeley delighted in polemical controversy, but he hated war. For more than a quarter of a century this strong thinker and master of the most vigorous English had furnished opinions to and done the thinking for vast masses of his fellow-citizens. In the anti-slavery movement, in the struggle for temperance legislation, in all moral reforms he was the most potent factor of his generation. Shocked and outraged beyond restraint when the first shot was fired at the flag, he demanded that the rebel soil be plowed with cannon balls and sown with salt, and his clarion notes rang through the land like a trumpet blast calling all loyal men to arms. But when he thought he saw a prospect of peace with slavery abolished, he recoiled appalled from further bloodshed and cried halt.

Unlike most strong natures, he harbored no resentments and was incapable of revenge. When the rebellion was crushed he went upon the bail bond of Jefferson Davis, as a protest against death penalties and confiscations, and in the hope of amnesty, reconciliation and brotherly reunion upon the basis won by our victory in the war. He so impressed and imbued Abraham Lincoln with his views that only the assassination of the President prevented their public announcement. He had been a devoted follower and passionate lover of Henry Clay, and three times had seen him set aside for the availability of military popularity. While most cordially conceding to General Grant position as the foremost Captain of his time, Mr. Greeley mistrusted his administrative ability in civil affairs, feared the result of his inexperience and intensely disliked his advisers. To President Grant, on the other hand, the great editor seemed something more and little less than an inspired crank. After the unfortunate results of some of the temporary and tentative State administrations in the South, Mr. Greeley conceived the idea that if the late rebels and slaveholders could be induced, in return for the full restoration of their State governments and universal amnesty, to accept the amendments to the Constitution, the freedom and citizenship of the slave, the inviolability of the debt and all the results of the war, with hearty loyalty to the flag waving over a Republic reconstructed on these conditions; and as hostage for their faith would take as their candidate for President a life-long abolitionist and Republican, the problem of reconstruction and peace would be solved at once. Responding to this idea the world beheld the amazing spectacle of these people, in convention assembled, solemnly declaring that the obligations of the Republic to the abolition of slavery, to the civil and po-

litical rights of the freedmen, to the honest
payment of the national debt, to the repudia-
tion of rebel loans, and to pensions to Union
soldiers, were unalterable and sacred, and then
nominating for President one who had said
more harsh and bitter things, and through his
writings and speeches done more effective work
for the overthrow of all their principles and
traditions, than any man living or dead. That
the South, without giving the evidences of
repentance then promised, has been granted
and now enjoys even more than Mr. Greeley
proposed, is the answer of the succeeding political generation to the fierce assaults made
at the time upon his theory and anticipations.
That a large majority of his party associates were
converted to his hopeful view at first, and
many followed him to the end, was natural,
when the movement was inspired and led by
so masterful and commanding an intellect which
had braved defeat and death for the rights of
men, and been always the first of the for-
lorn hope of liberty and reform, in the as-
sault upon the almost impregnable positions of
wrong, immorality and oppression for over a
quarter of a century. That he was defeated
and General Grant elected, the backward view
over the events since 1872, which is not diffi-

cult for most men to safely and correctly take,
proves to have been a wise and fortunate result. He was killed by his defeat. I stood
near as the clouds began to gather in that
active and mighty brain. He thought that a
life unselfishly given to mankind would be
judged a failure by posterity, and that the
fame which he had hoped would rest upon
the praise and gratitude of the humble and
oppressed, was already permanently injured by
the prejudices and distrust aroused in them by
the calumnies of the canvass. Though his controversies filled the land, this great fighter
for the truth as he understood it, was the
most morbidly sensitive of mortals, and weak-
ened by the sleepless strain of the struggle
and domestic affliction, his reason and life suc-
cumbed to ridicule and misrepresentation. We
have seen death in many forms, and for most
of us it has lost its terrors, but to witness a
great mind suddenly break and go out in help-
less and hopeless darkness was the saddest
scene I ever saw, and its memory is as of
the most painful of tragedies.

Horace Greeley was the last of that famous
triumvirate of editors, Greeley, Bennett and
Raymond, whose genius and individuality subordinated the functions of a great newspaper

to the presentation of their opinions and characteristics. Their journals were personal organs, but of phenomenal influence. The vigor of Mr. Greeley's thought and the lucidity of its expression, carried conviction to the minds of hundreds of thousands of people, and he was for nearly a quarter of a century the greatest individual force in the country. He was so honest and terrifically in earnest, so right in his motives and pure in his principles, that like the spots upon the sun, his mistakes made more evident the loftiness of his purposes. His motives were so transparent that his errors and eccentricities increased his strength, and even when wrong, he inspired more confidence than is reposed in most men when they are right. He made and unmade more reputations than any writer in the land. His untimely death hushed all hearts. President and Cabinet, generals and soldiers, Governors and Congressmen, friends and foes, the mighty and the humble, gathered at his bier, and the nation mourned as never before for the loss of a citizen in private station.

Mr. Fenton had acted with Mr. Greeley since the formation of the Republican party. They had been the closest of personal and political friends. They consulted freely and often on all questions and continued in fullest accord on party measures and policies.

After the dissolution of the famous partnership of Seward, Weed and Greeley, FENTON cast his fortunes with the junior member of the firm. His faith in Greeley and constant contact with his aspirations and views led to his full agreement with the opinions, and his fidelity to giving a cordial support to the ambitions of his friend.

PRIVATE LIFE AND CHARACTER.

After retiring from the Senate, Governor FENTON continued active and deeply interested in the success of his party, but was never again a candidate for office. President Hayes sent him abroad in 1878 as Chairman of the Commission to the International Monetary Convention to fix the ratio of value between gold and silver, and provide for their common use. But his health had become impaired by the strain of a busy and stormy life, and continued precarious until his sudden death while sitting at his office desk. The Governor and State officers, and a great multitude of people, representing the affection and respect of a large constituency, gave additional significance and solemnity to the last tributes to his memory.

REUBEN E. FENTON was remarkable for the full, rounded character of his mind and disposition. No matter how fiercely the storm raged about him he was always serene and unmoved. Though it was his fortunes which were at stake, he was the calmest of the combatants. He was the most affable and approachable of men, and yet until he acted none knew either his plans or his views. He listened courteously to every one, but what he heard rarely changed his deliberate judgment. In the heat of the contest, when upon his decision or signature depended results of the greatest importance to powerful and persistent applicants, his manner of receiving them led to angry charges that he had conveyed false impressions or been guilty of bad faith, but no proof was ever submitted, and it came to be admitted that he was simply, under the most tantalizing and exasperating conditions, always a gentleman. He was faultless in dress and manners, whether in the Executive Chamber, upon the platform or in the crowd, but this scrupulous exactness seemed to enhance his popularity. He loved to mingle freely with the people, but he received the like kindly greeting and cordial confidence from workingmen fresh from the forge, or mer-

chants in their parlors or counting-rooms.
When the history of our State comes to be
impartially written, Mr. FENTON will be given
rank as its best political organizer after Martin Van Buren. But he possessed a magnetism which Van Buren never had. A most
tender, gentle and affectionate nature shone
brightly for his friends through the crust of
the mannerisms of office and policy. I have
met all the public men of my time under
circumstances sufficiently close to form some
judgment as to the secrets of their power.
and he was one of the very few who had an
eloquent presence. His touch and look conveyed, if he pleased, such a world of interest
and regard, that the recipient, without know-
ing why, felt honored by his confidence and
encircled by his friendship. It was this which
made it impossible to crush him after repeated
defeats. When he was under the ban of
power, when to act with him was to accept
ostracism, when the office-holder was sure to
lose his place and the ambitious found all
avenues barred if they followed his lead, he
came year after year to the annual convention
of his party with such a solid, numerous and
aggressive host that it required all the resources of unsurpassed eloquence. political saga-

city and the lavish prizes of patronage to
prevent his carrying off the victory. The
character and deeds which redound to his
honor and will perpetuate his memory, are
sources of just pride for his State and of
lasting pleasure to his friends. He was a
representative of the people when the most
vital questions affecting the welfare of the
human race on this continent were at issue
and the Republic in the agonies of dissolution, and acted well the part of philanthro-
pist, patriot and statesman. He was twice
Governor of this State at a most critical
period in its history, wielding the powers of
the Executive with wisdom and courage, and
as the leader of the dominant party in the
Commonwealth, exercising a potent, but broad
and healthful influence in the affairs of the
Nation. He was United States Senator during the fruitful period of the reconstruction
of the government, and left enduring monu-
ments of his fidelity and ability as one of
the architects of the new era. As Congressman, Governor, Senator, there is no stain
upon his record, and his public life stands
pure and unassailed.

The controversies which occupied so large
a part of his life are over. The causes which

produced them have ceased to exist, and the friends and foes of that period can fight over the old battles without rancor or passion. The ever-dissolving and reuniting fragments of political forces wear off by friction enmities and jealousies, and by the recognition of merits before unknown in our opponents, we are all brought into more harmonious and respecting relations. We can all stand beside the grave of REUBEN E. FENTON, and forgetting for the moment our divisions and contentions, mourn the loss of one who in his day and generation acted so well his part as private citizen and public officer, that the Commonwealth and the country were enriched by his example, his character and his work.

CONCURRENT RESOLUTIONS

OF THE

SENATE AND ASSEMBLY.

STATE OF NEW YORK:

IN SENATE,

April 28, 1887.

Mr. VEDDER offered the following:

Resolved (it the Assembly concur), That there be printed under the direction of the Clerks of the Senate and Assembly, three thousand copies of the proceedings of this Legislature, and the memorial oration of the Hon. CHAUNCEY M. DEPEW, on the death of Ex-Governor REUBEN E. FENTON, for the use of the members of the Legislature, five hundred copies for the use of Mr. DEPEW, five hundred copies for the family of the deceased, and five hundred copies for the officers and reporters of the Legislature.

STATE OF NEW YORK:

IN SENATE,

The foregoing resolution was duly passed.

By order of the Senate.

JOHN W. VROOMAN,
Clerk.

STATE OF NEW YORK:

IN ASSEMBLY,

The foregoing resolution was duly concurred in.

By order of the Assembly.

CHAS. A. CHICKERING,
Clerk.

www.ingramcontent.com/pod-product-compliance
Lightning Source LLC
Chambersburg PA
CBHW030709110426
42739CB00031B/1367